It's the...

BUSY, NOISY, Snoozy, COSY,

cuddly, MUDDLY, LAZY, dozy,

slimy, grimy, crazy World of...

Acknowledgements
We would like to thank the Royal Veterinary College, London,
The Queen Mother Hospital for Animals, Hatfield,
and the PDSA in Bristol for their help.

Pets, Pets, Pets!

Kathy Henderson

Illustrated by Chris Fisher

MYRIAD BOOKS LIMITED

They're everywhere...

all over the place!
Where you'd least expect to see an *animal face*
appear, it's here. It's as STRANGE as it gets
but wherever there are **people**
there are sure to be **pets**!

White mice, hamsters, rabbits, **RATS**,
Horses, budgies, goldfish, **CATS**,
gerbils, guinea-pigs, ducks and **dogs**,
turtles, lizards, SNAKES and frogs,
spiders, SALAMANDERS, marmosets...

YES, wherever there are **people**
there are sure to be
Pets!

THE PET SHOP

Come in, come in, come in!

We've got
PALACES for hamsters four floors high,
cradles for cats to snooze in,
bean bags for dogs,
TERRARIUMS for frogs,
tanks for fish to cruise in.

We've got
STRAW and HAY, cat-litter trays,
tasty treats to chew on,
a collar and lead for every breed
and whatever FEED
you happen to need.

We've got
health food POTIONS, sun-tan lotions,
dog shampoos and pills.
And if YOU get a pet
we're ready to BET
You'll be putting YOUR money in our tills.

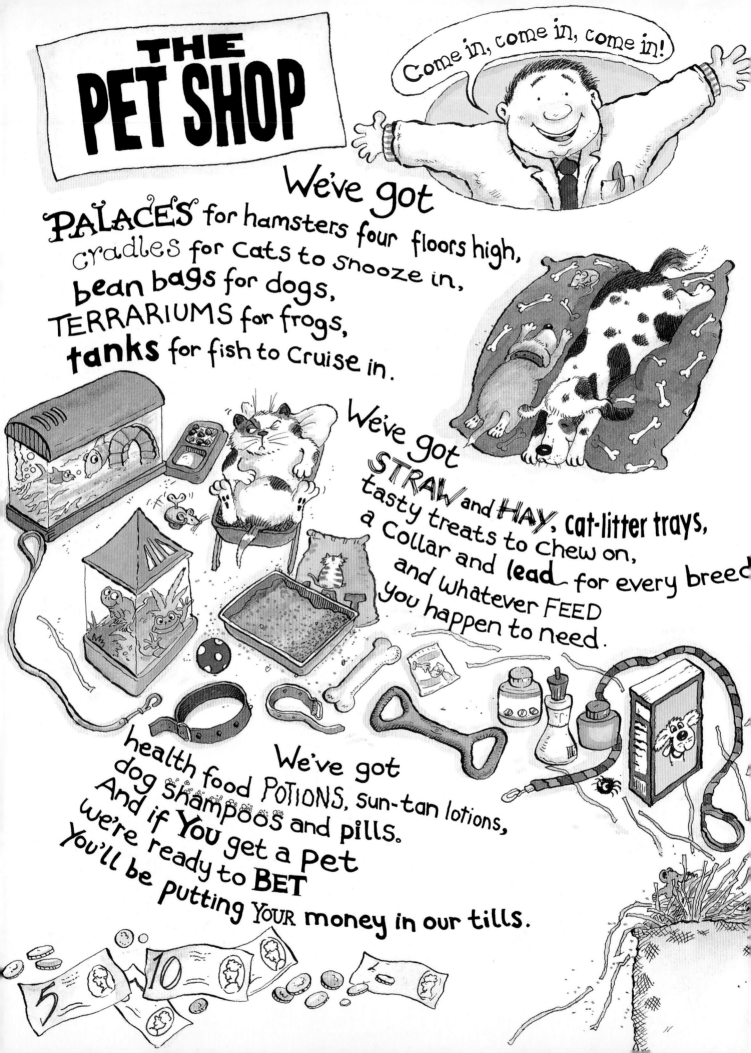

FEEDING TIME

Fido eats Wibblets and Tibbles likes titbits
and Crispin the Chicken eats slugs.
The white mice eat seeds, the rabbit eats weeds
and the cold dragon lizard eats bugs.

But then Tibbles decides in the blink of an eye
that she'd rather have lizard or Chicken or mice.
And Fido thinks slipper would taste rather nice...

And the white mice decide to escape from their cages
and shred up that armchair they've fancied for ages.
And Fido, who's mangled a slipper or two,
thinks a mouthful of CAT might be tasty to chew.
YES IT'S FEEDING TIME AT THE PET-LOVERS' ZOO
and who's to say who'll eat what?

HULLABALLOO!

DO THE POOPER-SCOOPER DOOP!

Boop-a-loop doop
Swoop on that poop!
Gloop-a-doop boop

You can do it on your own
You can do it in a group
Whistle and whoop
it's the pooper-scooper doop!

Just follow that dog
with your super-duper pooper-scooper.
Fill up that bag till you're ready to whoop.
Clean the cat-litter tray, take it away.
Muck out a horse as a matter of course.
Clean out those mice. YEAH! Done in a trice.
Free-range rabbit?

Dig that rabbit-droppings habit.

PRISCILLA'S POODLE PARLOUR

Priscilla's Poodle Parlour is the pleasantest of places
for grooming grubby greyhounds, Chihuahuas or dalmatians.
With a staff of six hostesses stocked with stunning SPECIAL skills
they know just how to put those perfect pooches through their paces

with a

Rover has his hairdo at a quarter to nine
— shampoo, clippers, brush, blow dry —
straighten his whiskers, trim his nails.
Isn't he handsome? Watch that tail!

Rover finds a mud patch
at a quarter to two.
Rolling in the dirt
is the ONLY thing to do.

Zadie has her hairdo at ten-fifteen
— bubble bath, towel dry, curl and preen —
on with her overcoat, tie that bow,
Zadie's ready for the Animal Show.

THE PET SHOW

There are CAT SHOWS, Horse Shows, Pig Shows, Dog Shows. For all I know there are beetle and FROG SHOWS.

Everybody brushed and dressed,
Every creature at its best,
Standing in that judging ring
doing the competition thing.

BUT...
What any pet knows
from the carthorse to the beetle
is that what shows
at pet shows
is really
Pet People.

Hide and Seek

Hide and seek— *bark purr squeak.*
Dig a hole, hide away,
    watch them all come out to play.

Here's a budgie on a lamppost
    and a cat stuck up a tree,
a ferret on a solo walk,
    a pet duck wandering— *quack and squawk,*
a lady on her hands and knees,
    searching for her pekinese,
a hamster underneath the floor
    and many, many, many more.

And here's the man from Rabbit Rescue
and the woman with the van
who rounds up straying chickens
and rehomes them if she can.
Here's the fire brigade come to the aid
of a big snake escapee
and someone sticking
RABBIT MISSING!
posters on the trees.

Yes it's Hide and Seek—
bark purr squeak.
This game happens
every day
BUT

RABBI
MISSI

WHY do we think that
pets should stay
where WE say
when THEY think
a different way?

WAITING FOR THE VET

We've come to see the vet,
We're waiting in the queue,
  a rabbit with a **swollen** JAW,
  a dog with something wrong with his PAW,
  a cat whose tummy's very sore,
All waiting for the vet.

We're waiting for the vet
To come and make things better,
  a parrot with a broken BEAK,
  a mouse that's gone and lost its SQUEAK,
  a snake that's feeling very weak,
All waiting for the vet.

We're waiting for her skills,
Injections, splints and pills.
  She's strong and sure and very WISE,
  She's got the right look in her EYES,
  She might just help us
    and that's why...

We're waiting for
the vet.

ANIMAL HOSPITAL

We rely on your donations

FLEAS! give him NO BITE!

PLEASE Report to Reception thanks

Help! Help! SOS!

A car's hurt **Fido**. **Fido's** in a mess!
The vet says **Fido's** very unwell,
take him to the animal hospital.

The surgeons and nurses
 X-ray and test him,
they wheel him into
 the operating theatre,
open him up and
 do their best.
Then they take him
 down to Intensive Care,
machines and nurses everywhere,
counting each breath.
 Will he make it? Who knows.
 It's touch and go   BUT...

A few days later on the ward
Fido's well enough to feel quite bored.

So now it's time for the therapy pool,
And lots of paddling
  to get him fit again.
And soon...

Fido's almost good as new.

Animal hospital,

THANK YOU
XXX

⋆∴MAGIC! ∴⋆

Oh the cat's had kittens and the ferret's had kits,
The fox has foxcubs and the budgie's hatched chicks,
The hedgehog's had hoglets and the dog's had pups:

⋆MAGIC! And we just lap it up.

There are holes in the carpet, toothmarks in the door,
Bucketfuls of mess, newspaper and straw,
There's cheeping in the bedroom,
   yapping in the hall:

MAGIC! And we just love it all.

Oh we cluck and we coo and we sit up all night,
We cuddle them and can't let them out of our sight,
We bore our friends and neighbours
    till their eyes go hazy:

MAGIC! We've gone animal crazy.

FASCINATING FACTS

HOW MANY?

★ Every other household in Britain has at least one pet! At the last count there were **6,500,000** dogs and **9,000,000** pet cats. That's more than one cat or dog for every child in the country. But...

★ Every year at least **27,000** dogs and **36,000** cats are found stray and unwanted.

★ In America, where there are **63,000,000** pet dogs and **64,000,000** pet cats, **8,000,000** cats and dogs have to be put down every year because they're lost or unwanted.

HOW MUCH?

★ Pets are big business. A pedigree kitten or puppy can cost as much as **£1,000**. In America **$1,000,000,000** is spent every year on doggie treats alone.

★ In Britain we spend **£1,500,000,000** on pet food every year. But...

★ Despite that, our pet cats still go out and kill around **275,000,000** voles, mice, birds, frogs and squirrels every year.

MORE...

★ A pair of rabbits can have up to **60 babies** in a single year. As for hamsters, in 1930 three Syrian hamsters produced a total of **364** babies in **365** days!

DID YOU KNOW?

★ There are pet portrait painters, luxury pet hotels, pet-sitters, pet sanctuaries, pet cemeteries, pet bereavement helplines, pet therapy groups, pet slimming clubs... You name it, they've got it!

OR...

★ If you don't fancy a live pet you can have a **robot** pet instead. A robot dog will only cost you between **£1,000** and **£20,000!**

MYRIAD BOOKS LIMITED
35 Bishopsthorpe Road, London SE26 4PA

First published in 2004 by
FRANCES LINCOLN LIMITED
4 Torriano Mews
Torriano Avenue
London NW5 2RZ

Pets, Pets, Pets! © Frances Lincoln Limited 2004
Text copyright © Kathy Henderson 2004
Illustrations copyright © Chris Fisher 2004
Hand lettering by Deborah Nash

ISBN 1 84746 002 X
EAN 9 781 84746 002 8
Printed in China